DUSTERS

TB

BRONZ

DCSKATEBOARDING
DCSKATEBOARDING

ALIEN
INVASION

Polaroid
LIGHT MANAGEMENT SYSTEM

RAZON

205

Penny

FOOD

GRIZZLY

POLIC
CINCINNATI
POLICE

etnies
etnies
etnies
etnies
etnies
etnies

ARBOR

Kahalani
BOOSTED

SKATEBOARD
LONDON

NIKE SB
Hurley

1965
KRYPTONICS
SKATEBOARDS

SB.

Made in the
USA
Middletown, DE

74009503R00035